THE SIGNIFICANCE
OF THE FRONTIER
IN AMERICAN HISTORY

978/1

Frederick Jackson Turner

THE SIGNIFICANCE OF THE FRONTIER IN AMERICAN HISTORY

Edited, with an introduction, by
HAROLD P. SIMONSON
University of Puget Sound

FREDERICK UNGAR PUBLISHING CO.
NEW YORK

MILESTONES
OF THOUGHT
in the History of Ideas

General Editors
HANS KOHN
The City College of New York
SIDNEY HOOK
New York University

195006

INTRODUCTION

A WRITER'S STATURE is often measured by the amount of controversy his ideas set in motion not only during his life but, even more importantly, years afterward. Among American historians past or present few have been more controversial than Frederick Jackson Turner who died in 1932 at the age of seventy-one. The storm broke at the very outset of his career when in 1893 the thirty-two-year-old historian appeared before the American Historical Association in Chicago and read to colleagues far more distinguished than himself his paper entitled "The Significance of the Frontier in American History." Listeners were not long in realizing that this relatively unknown professor from the University of Wisconsin had set off a bomb. And he had done it with this sentence: "The existence of an area of free land, its continuous recession, and the advance of American settlement westward, explain American development." Thus was born Turner's famous "frontier hypothesis."

That Turner's hypothesis continues to be one of the major controversies in American historical study attests to the importance of the man. Only one other historian, Francis Parkman, challenges his eminence; from the viewpoint of many scholars Turner stands alone. Benjamin F. Wright, Jr., called him "the most brilliant and most influential of American historians"; John D. Hicks thought that "what Turner had to say probably no one else will ever be able to say as well." More recently, Merle Curti has said that in "originality" and "influence," Frederick Jackson Turner "has thus far had no superior if he has had any peer." [1]

[1] Benjamin F. Wright, Jr., "Political Institutions and the Frontier," in Dixon Ryan Fox (ed.), *Sources of Culture in the Middle West: Backgrounds versus Frontier* (New York, 1934), p. 16; John D. Hicks, "The Development of Civilization in the Middle West, 1860–1900," in Fox, *ibid.*, p. 75; Merle Curti, *Probing Our Past* (New York, 1955), p. 32.

By far the most important piece he wrote was "The Significance of the Frontier in American History." For what this essay says about the American identity ranks it with Emerson's great essay, "The American Scholar." Both were declarations of independence, both asserted that the uniqueness of American institutions largely evolved from the national experience itself, not from traditions inherited from Europe. One listener in Turner's Chicago audience called his paper "the Monroe Doctrine of American historical writing." Dixon Ryan Fox later called it "the most famous and most influential paper in American historiography." "No other academic statement," Professor Fox said, "had had comparable effect on this side of the Atlantic." Ray Allen Billington has recently pointed out that Turner's hypothesis in this essay was transformed "into not *one*, but *the* explanation of American history." In short, what we have is an amazingly influential account of our national development seen from a Westerner's point of view.[2]

Of course Turner was not the first to call attention to the significance of the Western frontier. Thomas Jefferson long before had realized that the West would have an important role in shaping the new nation. In 1829 this fact was irrefutably established when Andrew Jackson moved into the White House. But the significance of the fact was less obvious. Timothy Dwight, President of Yale, saw no reason in 1821 to take Western expansion seriously. To him pioneers were merely social misfits—"too idle, too talkative, too passionate, too prodigal, and too shiftless to acquire either property or character." Another dyed-in-the-wool New Englander, Oliver Wendell Holmes, found amusement in comparing a typical Boston Brahmin with his "inelegant," "uncouth," "coarse," and "clumsy" counterpart in the West.

[2] Avery Craven, "Frederick Jackson Turner," in William T. Hutchinson (ed.), *The Marcus W. Jernegan Essays in American Historiography* (New York, 1937), p. 254; Dixon Ryan Fox, "Editor's Explanation," in Fox, *op. cit.*, p. 3; Ray Allen Billington (ed.), *Frontier and Section: Selected Essays of Frederick Jackson Turner* (Englewood Cliffs, N.J., 1961), p. 6.

Other writers like Henry W. Longfellow and Washington Irving or the lesser known Timothy Flint and James Hall romanticized the West but failed to appreciate its broad influence in American development. James Fenimore Cooper mythologized it by creating Natty Bumppo, the archetypal man, who represented the best of both possible worlds— Eastern civilization and Western primitiveness. But whatever one's point of view, one thing became clear: by the second half of the nineteenth century the West could not be ignored. The free-soil issue in Abraham Lincoln's 1860 campaign clearly warned the New England capitalists that Western interests now rivaled their own special ones in the East. Passage of the important Homestead Act in 1862 left no doubt that the call "Go west, young man" would influence American life for years to come. Central to Turner's hypothesis is that this westward movement into the primitive areas lying always beyond the frontier was *the* significant fact in the American identity.[3]

II

One year before the Homestead Act, Frederick Jackson Turner was born in Portage, Wisconsin, the heartland of what was then the Old Northwest. His parents had left upper New York state to settle in this small frontier town, the site of Old Fort Winnebago which John Jacob Astor had built as a fur trading post. Being a journalist and local historian, Andrew Jackson Turner excited his son's imagination with Wisconsin history and, of course, with the special lore surrounding Portage. There were the stories of the Winnebagoes, the trappers and fur traders, the loggers, and then the Wisconsin River itself which to the Indians meant "black rushing water." It is not surprising that Turner's master's thesis, written at the University of Wisconsin in

[3] Timothy Dwight, *Travels in New-England and New-York* (1821– 1822); Oliver Wendell Holmes, *Elsie Venner: A Romance of Destiny* (1861).

1888, should be on Wisconsin history, specifically, "The Influence of the Fur Trade in the Development of Wisconsin."

After first earning his bachelor's degree in 1884 at the State university, he worked as a journalist in Madison for only a year before deciding to return to the university. He chose to study history under William Francis Allen who painstakingly taught him the scholar's code to examine sources, to winnow truth from error, and then after sufficient inquiry to arrive at forceful and significant conclusions. This rigor suited Turner's intellectual temperament and in later years led to his writing the kind of history that required vast generalizations concerned with the meanings of events.

After he left Wisconsin in 1888 with a Master of Arts degree, he studied at Johns Hopkins University in Baltimore under the sociologist Albion Small and such notable historians as Woodrow Wilson, Richard T. Ely, and Herbert Baxter Adams. The climate of historical research at Johns Hopkins centered on Professor Adams' "germ theory" which accounted for historic change in terms of antecedents or "germs." This theory explained American institutions in terms of European influences dating as far back as the Teutonic tribes of the Middle Ages. This interpretation resembled that of American literary scholars who at this same time were seeking to link American development with an Anglo-Saxon heritage while discounting peculiarly native elements. Adams' theory served as a kind of negative catalyst to Turner who, because of it, grew even more steadfast in his opposition to the notion that heredity comprised a stronger influence than environment. He could hardly account for the history of his own state of Wisconsin in terms of European "germs." For his doctoral dissertation he once again studied regional history, enlarging his earlier master's thesis into a monograph entitled "The Character and Influence of the Indian Trade in Wisconsin: A Study of the Trading Post as an Institution." Though he made some concessions to Professor Adams by tracing fur trading back to the ancient world, Turner clearly showed that frontier conditions unique only to Wisconsin shaped its fur trading industry. Upon this environmental interpretation of history Turner rested his case.

In 1891 he returned as professor of history to the University of Wisconsin where he remained for the next nineteen years. Of his many students none wrote more sensitively about him than Carl Becker who also became a prominent historian. Recalling his graduate student days, Becker wrote that Turner had "a singular capacity for making you want to do and be something—to do, in short, what he was doing, and to be, if possible, what he was." Always engaged in research, Turner drew students to him who were interested in his interests; and, wrote Becker, they had "the inestimable privilege of watching an original and penetrating intelligence at work." [4] Avery Craven, another student who later became a professional historian, observed with telling logic that because Turner was "never particularly interested in teaching per se, he thereby became a great teacher." [5]

Turner was content in Wisconsin. His gold mine was the State Historical Society library, better equipped in American history than any library west of the Allegheny Mountains. Here were the fur-trader manuscripts he had earlier used, and here too were the materials supporting his theory of American history. At the University of Wisconsin his scholarly output was not large. Craven noted that Turner wrote less yet influenced more students than any other important historian. Throughout his career he wrote no more than thirty major essays some of which he collected in *The Frontier in American History* (1920) and others in *The Significance of Sections in American History* (1932).

[4] Carl L. Becker, "Frederick Jackson Turner," in *Everyman His Own Historian: Essays on History and Politics* (New York, 1935), pp. 191–232.

[5] Craven, p. 267.

In 1906 appeared his first book entitled *The Rise of the New West 1819–1829*. He worked for the rest of his life on a second book which was to continue the frontier story to 1850. While engaged in it he died. Three years afterward, in 1935, the uncompleted manuscript was edited by Professor Craven and published as *The United States, 1830–1850: The Nation and Its Sections*.

The nineteen years at the University of Wisconsin mark his most creative period, not in terms of published work but rather in terms of creative thought. It was the period in which he formulated his monumental frontier hypothesis which, in turn, led to important theories about sectionalism, nationalism, and democracy. In 1910 he left Wisconsin for a professorship at Harvard where he stayed until 1924. Nothing he did during this period eclipsed his already brilliant work. Because of poor health he went to Pasadena, California, where he worked as a research associate at the great Huntington Library until his death in March 1932.

III

It is exciting to go back and follow Turner during those first three years as a young professor at Wisconsin: to see him start to formulate his central ideas and then within only three years to write the essay which transformed American historiography.

In his first year he published "The Significance of History," a major essay which reveals his early enthusiasm for the historian's high calling. "*Sursum corda,* lift up your hearts," he wrote as an invocation to all historians who would enter the "temple of history." History, he said, is nothing less than "the self-consciousness of humanity." The historian's materials include all that remains of the past; his job is to gather, sift, and evaluate these materials and also to search for the large sweeping principles behind external events.

Turner viewed history as organic, ever growing, with

its present roots lying deep in the past. This outlook required that the historian not only reconstruct the many facets of the past but interpret the present in terms of the past. In this same essay he eloquently announced: "Each age writes the history of the past anew with reference to the conditions uppermost in its own time." History was not something static or definitive, as he thought Adams' "germ theory" to suggest. In claiming that there was no such thing as a definitively written history, he called for a much broader historical perspective which would include, above all, the constantly changing environmental factors. This meant that the historian's new tools would include geography, geology, biology, meteorology, sociology, economics, literature, religion. He would replace old books on political history with present-day maps and statistics. With Emerson he might have said, "Our day of dependence, our long apprenticeship to the learning of other lands, draws to a close." Henceforth, the American historical scholar is to redirect his attention to his own civilization.

Turner also saw the need for specialization: "Select some field and till that thoroughly, be absolute master of it." In Turner's second major essay, written during his second year as professor at Wisconsin, he more than hinted what his own life-long specialization would be. In this essay, entitled "Problems in American History," he pointed out that American history needs "a connected and unified account." He was convinced that the fundamental fact in American history was not Puritan New England, the conflict between Northern industrialists and Southern agrarians, nor the economic warfare between industry and labor in his own day. It was instead the progress of civilization from the Alleghenies to the Pacific. "This ever retreating frontier of free land," he wrote in 1892, "is the key to American development." Like Emerson, Turner had first sounded his independence from Europe. Now, like Mark Twain, he declared his independence from the East coast and especially from its tradition-bound universities.

Turner's palpable excitement, his sense of mission, was contagious among his students. In this second essay is a cascade of subjects relevant to the West which Turner said needed research: a marvelous boon to graduate students setting out to write their papers. Turner's surging rhetoric suggests that he himself could complete the grand design of American history had he only world enough and time. The essay makes clear that Turner was on the verge of something big, something which was speedily taking shape in his mind and which soon had to be said.

His next essay the following year was the decisive one. In "The Significance of the Frontier in American History" Turner put down his remarkably mature explanation of the West's role in American history. His later influence as a historian was largely measured by this essay, not a word of which he changed when he republished it twenty-seven years later in *The Frontier in American History*. It is true that his frontier hypothesis was not his only significant contribution. Some historians believe that his later theory on geographic sections was more important. But it was specifically this 1893 essay that skyrocketed Turner into uneclipsed eminence.

IV

Turner carefully began this famous essay by announcing the startling fact that America no longer had a frontier. Quoting the statement of the Superintendent of the Census of 1890 which reported the disappearance of a "frontier line," Turner went on to explain that the disappearance of the frontier signaled the end "of a great historic movement." Population in the West had reached the figure of at least two persons per square mile, the basis for calling an area settled. No land now remained which could be designated as unsettled. Therefore, that vaguely determined line—the frontier—separating these two areas had vanished. Not to let his audience forget this fact, he dramatically reiterated it at the end of the essay, even implying a world-wide relevance by noting that the closing of the frontier occurred on the four-hundredth anniversary of Columbus' discovery.

For one to appreciate the vast significance Turner placed upon the passing of the frontier, it is necessary to understand his interpretation of the frontier itself. Far more than a geographic or statistical fact, the frontier divided the primitive from the civilized; it distinguished the natural from the institutional, the savage from the cultured, the elemental from the complex. Where the two met, there was the frontier which worked a metabolic change upon both. Inevitably, however, the former gave way to the latter. Though at first the wilderness mastered the pioneer, the pioneer slowly transformed the wilderness. According to Turner this process was the ultimately significant fact in American history. In first being overwhelmed by nature, then in overwhelming it, the pioneer underwent a process which "Americanized" him. It freed him from dependence upon Europe. It made him not only a more self-conscious American but, as Turner emphasized, a more self-conscious Westerner. The frontier transformed his old ways into new American ways, and subduing nature became the American's manifest destiny.

The titanic struggle between man and nature symbolized something even bigger than the strictly American story. To Turner it appeared as an epic re-enacting the story of mankind, both past and present. "Stand at Cumberland Gap," he wrote, "and watch the procession of civilization, marching single file—the buffalo following the trail to the salt springs, the Indian, the fur trader and hunter, the cattle raiser, the pioneer farmer." The "procession of civilization" dramatized man's triumph over nature and the coming of enlightenment. Where originally there had been only a "simple, inert continent" the advancing frontier left behind "a complex nervous system." All this to Turner represented progress, a notion dear to the nineteenth century.

Turner's metaphors intensify the drama. Gold discoveries in California sent a "sudden tide" of adventurers west. The frontier earlier "had leaped" over the Alleghenies; now it "skipped," "passed in successive waves," "stretched" like a "cord of union." Among historians only Henry Nash Smith has paid more than incidental attention to Turner's dazzling rhetoric, though Professor Smith is somewhat alarmed in finding that Turner's metaphors "threaten to become themselves a means of cognition and to supplant discursive reasoning." [6] It is, of course, Turner's use of metaphor which gives his ideas such compelling power. Metaphor is essential to his conception: what once was an "inert continent" is now, metaphorically, an awakened organism—its "nervous system" alive, changing, growing, evolving.

The American frontier, then, was far more than a line on a map. It was a process in which men first confronted and then mastered their raw environment. With each succeeding wave of immigrants the process grew more complex. Behind the hunters and fur traders came the cattlemen, then the farmers who tilled and fenced the land, then the industrial workers. Each group had its own frontier to master, the whole process entailing mastery of successive frontiers. Out of what Turner called "inert" nature grew a society, a nation, and a civilization. Moving his eye from east to west, he saw the drama unfold into a uniquely American "nervous system."

Turner was not yet done with metaphor in this essay. He described the American process in terms of a continual "return" to the primitive and elemental, a "perennial rebirth." Each time the frontier advances, the original encounter between civilization and the wilderness is recapitulated and the original challenges are again to be met. The consequence pertains not only to a new nation but to a new kind of man, a transformation of human nature. Stripped of his accumulations the settler is forced to become selfsufficient. Each new start on an advancing frontier develops

[6] Henry Nash Smith, *Virgin Land: The American West as Symbol and Myth* (Harvard University Press, 1950), p. 254.

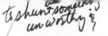
to shunt something unworthy?

in him "stalwart and rugged qualities." A foremost individualist, he eschews both authority and society if he feels choked by them. Restless, inventive, self-confident, optimistic, enormously energetic—such qualities as these Turner found nurtured with each renewal of the frontier experience. Like America's arch romantics, Henry David Thoreau and Walt Whitman, Turner vaguely felt some occult power in nature which liberated a man from pettiness and enabled him to grow to his full measure. Thoreau's experience at Walden Pond was a ritual of rebirth, as was Whitman's which he described in "Crossing Brooklyn Ferry" and "Passage to India." From these experiences came a personality new-born in the knowledge not only that he was participating in a grand design but also that he was the agent shaping it, fulfilling it. All this gigantic transformation Turner linked with the new American and the new democratic man. Three years later in his essay, "The Problem of the West," Turner sang hosannas about the frontiersman as prophet who "dreamed dreams and beheld visions." The archetype was America's greatest mythical hero, Abraham Lincoln, whom Turner called "the very flower of frontier training and ideals."

Clearly, the significance of the frontier to Frederick Jackson Turner reached far and wide. The frontier led to the formation of a "composite nationality"; it decreased our dependence on England; it brought on various internal improvements such as railroads and agriculture; it played a vital part in legislation dealing with tariffs, land distribution, and improvements. But its most important effect, according to Turner, was in "the promotion of democracy" seen especially in frontier individualism.

Implicit in Turner's concept of democracy is the individual, the transformed man. This romantic figure combines both frontier mysticism and executive know-how. He finds essential values in both primitive and urban societies. He transcends the grossness of the frontier and the inhumanity of industrialism. In short, he is the perfected man whose frontier training has made him successful in modern America.

Turner's visions were not without misgivings. He saw that rugged individualism born of free land may lead more to selfishness than civic-mindedness. For example, he associated lax business integrity with the kind of frontier liberty which had stretched beyond its proper bounds. The truth is that Turner saw the difficulty in reconciling a perennial rebirth of innocence with the ethics of business. "A primitive society," he said, "can hardly be expected to show intelligent appreciation of the complexity of business interests in a developed society." With the same logic he could have written that business interests can hardly appreciate a beneficial return to primitive, mystic experience. Either way Turner was caught in crucial ambiguities. The American was to control nature and yet be receptive to its occult power. He was to merge into a complex society and yet maintain his individual integrity, to work for the common good and yet seek individual gain. To resolve these tensions Turner created a mythical American in whom both extremes coalesced. His ideal was the perennial romantic who remained untainted amid the widespread problems of a new industrial society.

Another concept in Turner's famous essay needs to be noted. This is his "safety-valve" theory, significantly juxtaposed in the last paragraph with the reiterated announcement that the frontier is now closed. According to Turner the frontier had served as a safety valve for all the discontents who were trapped either by past customs or by present economic hardships. The availability of free land to the west supposedly allowed them to break away. At the frontier, Turner said, "the bonds of custom are broken and unrestraint is triumphant." The implications are of course immense. If oppressed or defeated, a person needed only to go west and start over again. At the frontier all men had an equal chance. Success belonged to the strongest who by his own sweat wrested a new livelihood from the land.

Symbolically associated with the frontier were such entice-
ments as open roads and new horizons. Nineteenth century
American literature is full of this kind of promise which,
at the turn of the century, was attacked by such literary
realists as Stephen Crane and Theodore Dreiser who
stressed man's social, economic, and spiritual entrapment.
Frederick Jackson Turner, however, remained firmly rooted
in the safety-valve promise which, according to Professor
Smith, was Turner's "imaginative construction" masking
"poverty and industrial strife." [7]

Turner did not tackle these new problems. Though he
lived over thirty years into the twentieth century, his main
historical concerns ended with the closing of the frontier.
Many critics of Turner feel that his study ought to have
included more extensive treatment of the years following
the frontier's closing. But he remained an historian of the
nineteenth century American West. As such, he did not
plunge into such issues as labor agitation and the rise of
unions, American expansion abroad, laissez-faire capitalism,
government control, and social reform. He centered his
attention on the frontier and the sectional configurations
shaped by the people living within them.

On the other hand it would be inaccurate to say that
Turner totally ignored the consequences implied in his mo-
mentous announcement that the frontier or safety valve had
closed. The juxtaposition in his last paragraph is too skill-
fully handled for the reader to miss Turner's anxiety. America was clearly at a turning point and Turner knew it. One
thinks of another historian whose anxiety about the direction of American history pivoted around the year 1893. In
that year Henry Adams saw the immense dynamos exhibited at the Chicago World's Fair, and to him they symbolized all the disintegration and multiplicity of the oncoming
century. Turner's intransigent optimism shielded him from
the cosmic and tragic sense which darkened Adams' pro-

[7] *Ibid.*, pp. 205–206.

phetic vision so powerfully put forth in *The Education of Henry Adams.*

Turner's closest look at the new century, bereft of a frontier, is the 1903 essay, "Contributions of the West to American Democracy," and another essay entitled "Social Forces in American History" published seven years later. In the first one he briefly reviewed the ten years following his 1893 announcement. He found this period strangely revolutionary. With the supply of free land exhausted the Western movement, he said, could no longer constitute "an effective factor" in American growth. Furthermore, the concentration of wealth among only a few industrialists had opened a serious cleavage between capital and labor. Another phenomenon was American political and commercial expansion abroad. And a final revolutionary change was "the birth of new political ideas," specifically the socialistic views of the Populist party led by William Jennings Bryan. Discussion of similar topics comprised the second essay, "Social Forces in American History": the gain of socialism and new political party lines; industrialism; American world politics; demands for primary elections and suffrage legislation; and, strangest of all, the fact that these new social forces were emerging in regions where once frontier democracy reigned supreme.

Though Turner encouraged his students to explore these issues, the master himself stayed with the past. In so doing he never satisfactorily answered the logical imputation that when America lost its frontier it also lost its wellspring of democracy. Even with the frontier gone Turner never argued that America no longer had a vital democratic source. He believed that the democratic ideals engendered on the frontier had sufficient momentum to continue. Professing his faith and unflagging romanticism in this 1903 essay, he quoted Rudyard Kipling's poem, "Song of the English," which begins, "We were dreamers, dreaming greatly," and then continues, "Came the Whisper, came the Vision, came the Power with the Need." What Turner intended to

show in this essay was that the disappearance of the frontier
did not mean the end of democracy. He insisted that the
fine flower of modern civilization—industrialism—actually
corroborated democratic principles. He went even further
by calling the new industrialists "pathfinders for democracy," "great geniuses" who inherited the old frontier spirit
and still professed its ideals. Turner's roll call included
John D. Rockefeller, Marcus Hanna, Claus Spreckles, Mar-
shall Field, Andrew Carnegie—all Horatio Algers taking
their cue from Carnegie's words, which Turner admiringly
quoted: "Thank God, these treasures are in the hands of an
intelligent people, the Democracy." To the question—
Whither American democracy?—Turner's remarkable answer
came with clarion power: "Let us see to it that the ideals
of the pioneer in his log cabin shall enlarge into the spiritual
life of a democracy where civic power shall dominate and
utilize individual achievement for the common good."

Triumph of spiritual life hardly describes the decade
following Turner's 1903 utterance. Many Americans thought
a more accurate picture was to be found in Lincoln Steffens'
The Shame of the Cities (1904), Upton Sinclair's *The Jun-
gle* (1906), and Jane Addams' *Twenty Years at Hull House*
(1910). Readers were hard pressed to discover beneficent
ideals embodied in the American civilization which these
books described. Consequently they were prepared for Alfred North Whitehead's pronouncement several years later
that "instead of dwelling on the brotherhood of man," modern civilization was now directed "to procure the extermina-
tion of the unfit." [8] Rampant practices of laissez-faire capitalism, protected under a democratic guise, had brutalized
life to the point where many disillusioned intellectuals re-
placed their log cabin ideologies with Marxist ones from
abroad.

Turner's faith in rugged individualism and man's inherent goodness remained unshaken. In "The West and

[8] Alfred North Whitehead, *Adventures of Ideas* (New York, 1933),
pp. 44–45.

American Ideals," an essay published in 1914, he still insisted that frontier idealism dominated American life. "From the beginning," he wrote, "America has never been the home of mere contented materialism." He saw no reason for America now to lose its frontier spirit: "Let us dream as our fathers dreamt and let us make our dreams come true." Turner's dream was of a "perfected social type" directed by the ideals of discovery, democracy, and individualism, and completely hospitable to a climate of free competition in which the highest achievements in business, arts, letters, and science went to the strongest. His utopian dream calling for "new and nobler achievements" was to be upheld by "the Western spirit" which Turner found expressed in Tennyson's dog-eared poem, "Ulysses," containing the favorite line: "To strive, to seek, to find and not to yield."

According to Turner the most ominous threat to the frontier spirit came not from the rumblings of war just beginning in Europe but from excessive governmental power at home. Without specifying the Progressives led by Robert M. LaFollette, who also hailed from Wisconsin, Turner obviously had them in mind. Coming from their ranks were demands for free silver, public ownership of agencies of communication and transportation, credit for agriculture, and extended voting rights. Turner implied that Americans, especially the Western pioneers, had "deserted" their earlier spirit of competitive individualism in order to attain these reforms which contradicted laissez-faire attitudes. In full view of rapidly changing times Turner insisted that the old frontier heritage would remain a permanent and inviolable bequest to the future.

V

Turner's frontier hypothesis remained virtually unchallenged during the twenty-five years following his 1893 essay. Many of his former students at Wisconsin and Harvard continued the job of interpreting American democracy in terms of his original theories about the significance of the West. But with the widespread disenchantment which followed World War I other historians grew restless with what seemed to them Turner's antiquated ideas. By the 1930's they leveled a tremendous barrage against him. Louis M. Hacker wrote in *The Nation* that another generation of historical scholars will be needed to destroy Turner's fabrications which were not only "fictitious" but "positively harmful." [9] Even today the pros and cons continue to debate. Some historians think that Turner's thesis is dead; others believe it still lucidly explains both nineteenth and twentieth century American development and our national ideals.

Critics have attacked Turner on at least five points. First of all they say that his thesis was too simple, that in emphasizing the American West he overlooked such powerful groups as the Southern agrarians, Eastern capitalists, and Middle Western Progressives. Carl Becker, Turner's illustrious student, thought it unaccountable that he had disregarded these other groups. Some critics have suggested that instead of studying Wisconsin fur trade, Turner should have been investigating the claims of Progressivism in his home state and reading such books as Henry Demarest Lloyd's *Wealth Against Commonwealth* or A. T. Mahon's *The United States Looking Outward*. In short, readers have felt that Turner pushed his thesis too far in trying to explain American development solely in terms of Western influence.

Turner's efforts to homogenize a complex American society into a "composite nationality" disturbed still others who argued that merely because people are subjected to the same frontier environment, assuming that they are, is no reason to suppose that all will be transformed into stereotyped Americans. Turner's environmentalism seemed to them little else than materialistic determinism which overemphasized geographic and climatic factors and disregarded

[9] Louis M. Hacker, "Sections—or Classes?" *The Nation*, CXXXVII (July 26, 1933), 108.

both European backgrounds and inherent free will. In fact, a serious contradiction does occur when Turner's theory of "composite nationality" is juxtaposed with his later theory of sectionalism by which he described physiographic sections—the Middle Atlantic, New England, South Atlantic, Middle West, Far West—in terms of the heterogeneity of the immigrants. Professor Craven noted that "Turner went on insisting in the nationalizing force of the frontier and describing the thoroughly sectional character of the results." [10]

Another point of attack was aimed at the safety-valve theory. According to Turner the availability of free land had given the working man a chance to fulfill his dreams of independence, because on his 160 acres granted under the Homestead Act any sturdy yeoman could make his own way. Unfortunately the myth was not sustained by actualities; and, as Professor Smith has shown, what was anticipated as a garden often turned out to be a desert, both literally and figuratively. Droughts in the Great Plains sent many homesteaders back again to the Middle West and East. Unscrupulous land speculators and railroad monopolists forced their demands upon the unorganized farmers. In many instances the farmer was no freer than the penniless mill worker. To use Hamlin Garland's term, both were under "the lion's paw." Turner's safety-valve theory had seemed to discount the fact that by 1890 twenty-four percent of all American farmers were tenants on somebody else's land. Ten years later the figure had risen to thirty-five percent.

The last two charges against Turner carried the most weight because they struck at the heart of his thesis. Throughout his career he believed that free land and the westward movement "explain" American development. In his 1896 essay, "The Problem of the West," he claimed that the backwoodsmen's "forest philosophy is the philosophy of

[10] Craven, p. 257.

American democracy." In one of his most celebrated statements, this one from his 1914 essay on "The West and American Ideals," he asserted that American democracy was not brought to Virginia in the *Sarah Constant* nor to Plymouth in the *Mayflower* but was born in "the American forest." Serious questions immediately arise: Was the growth of American democracy isolated from the course of Western civilization? Does the frontier "explain" the American industrial revolution or American music, architecture, literature, religion? "Above all," asked Professor George Pierson, "what happens to intellectual history if the environment be all?" [11] The fact that most American statesmen had thorough training in European background would suggest that American democracy did indeed have "germs." For example, Alexander Hamilton without Hobbes or Thomas Jefferson without Rousseau would be unimaginable. To discount our intellectual inheritance would lead only to nativism and isolationism, and this outcome Turner's critics considered especially dangerous in view of America's inexperience in world leadership, a role which after World War I she accepted. Historian Percy Boynton answered Turner's forest philosophy by quoting Sinclair Lewis' Dodsworth: "Our adventure [in America] is going to be the bigger because we *do* feel that Europe has a lot we need. We're no longer satisfied with the log cabin and the corn pone. We want everything that Europe has. We'll take it." [12]

The most serious charge has been directed against Turner's concept of democracy. His whole thesis rests on the assumption that in this ideology is a certain mystique, a spiritual essence by which persons can achieve their full measure of individuality and dignity. But once again serious questions arise: By democracy did Turner mean equalitari-

[11] George W. Pierson, "The Frontier and American Institutions: A Criticism of the Turner Theory," *New England Quarterly,* XV (June, 1942), 224.

[12] Percy H. Boynton, *The Rediscovery of the Frontier* (University of Chicago Press, 1931), p. 185.

anism? Or did he mean something akin to social Darwinism whereby in unrestricted competition the strong become stronger? To what extent was individual freedom to be controlled by legislation? How did Turner's concept of democracy speak to such issues as suffrage, denied to all American women until 1920; to race and class exploitation; and, in fact, to what now many Americans consider the most important nineteenth century issue—freedom for the Negro slaves? Turner's failure to give adequate answers convinced many historians that while Turner's covered wagon may have been hitched to Emerson's star it certainly was not in touch with mundane realities. Turner's claim, for example, that the frontiersman experienced some kind of mystical rebirth hardly jibed with the picture of restless and usually undignified claim-holders employing any means to get rich quicker.

VI

Summarizing the arguments which swirl around Turner leads one to the careful words of Merle Curti who, after surveying the many theories and sources of our American institutions, concluded that "there has been no consensus about either the meaning of American democracy or its origins and conditioning circumstances or the degree of importance it has had in our national experience." [13] What can be said, however, is that as long as questions are still open and answers are still supplied then challenged, American democracy regardless of its definition will remain operative.

As for Turner's famous 1893 essay, it marks a significant point in American historiography not only because of Turner's research methods but also because of his choice of subjects to investigate. Furthermore, at a time when Amer-

[13] Curti, p. 29.

icans were growing more conscious of their "usable past," Turner's efforts to identify and describe it sent many other historians forth to do the same. Some of them expanded his thesis; others rejected it and established their own. Catalytic as Turner's synthesis was, his own certainty that America had an identifiable and unique civilization made an even greater impact which he sustained by indefatigably describing the native origins comprising it.

His frontier thesis was undoubtedly too simple. Yet no historian has effectively argued that there is *no* relationship between American democracy and the frontier. That the frontier was significant in American development is a fact which still stands unrefuted. Another fact equally inviolable is that Turner's 1893 essay is one of our best documents revealing a basic 19th century American attitude. In a sense Turner was no rebel at all, even though he opposed his Johns Hopkins professors. What he did was to perpetuate the American dream which first flowered in early 19th century New England. Though Turner used the methods of a pragmatist, he would have been at home among the Concord idealists. Basic to his theories is the belief, like that of the Transcendentalists, that man and nature harmoniously interact because behind both is a common spiritual reality. Such a notion inspires faith in the goodness of both man and nature and faith in an ever expanding frontier which leaves in its wake compelling evidence of human progress.

This American dream went underground at the turn of the century. Many observers said that the nation's newly created industrial society turned nature into a plundered wasteland and robbed man of spirit and dignity. The argument continued, especially in American literature, that the American obsession to master and to possess nature transformed our self-sufficiency into pride which then led to the psychological and theological consequences of both guilt and sin. Despite these dire observations, the original dream which went underground is far from extinguished. The word "frontier" still plays a significant part in our national ideology especially now that the frontier has become three-dimensional. And Frederick Jackson Turner still is remembered as the historian who first so dynamically called attention to this significance.

SELECTED BIBLIOGRAPHY

Turner's main essays are collected in *The Frontier in American History* (New York, 1920) and *The Significance of Sections in American History* (New York, 1932). His two other books are *Rise of the New West, 1819–1829* (New York, 1906) and *The United States, 1830–1850: The Nation and Its Sections* (New York, 1935). For a complete bibliography of Turner's writings students should consult *The Early Writings of Frederick Jackson Turner, With a List of All His Works*, Compiled by Everett E. Edwards and an Introduction by Fulmer Mood (University of Wisconsin Press, 1938).

Scholarly assessment of Turner is extensive. In addition to the works mentioned in the footnotes, the following items dealing with Turner's frontier theory are especially recommended:

Ray Allen Billington, *Westward Expansion: A History of the American Frontier* (New York, 1949), ch. 11.

Stanley Elkins and Eric McKitrick, "A Meaning for Turner's Frontier, Part I: Democracy in the Old Northwest," *Political Science Quarterly*, LXIX (September, 1954), 323–339.

Carlton J. H. Hayes, "The American Frontier—Frontier of What?" *American Historical Review*, LI (January, 1946), 199–210, 216.

Richard Hofstadter, "Turner and the Frontier Myth," *American Scholar*, XVIII (October, 1949), 433–443.

James C. Malin, "Space and History: Reflections on the Closed-Space Doctrines of Turner and Mackinder and the Challenge of Those Ideas by the Air Age," *Agricultural History*, XVIII (April, 1944), 65–74.

Herman C. Nixon, "Precursors of Turner in the Interpretation of the American Frontier," *South Atlantic Quarterly*, XXVIII (January, 1929), 83–89.

Frederick L. Paxson, "A Generation of the Frontier Hypothesis: 1893–1932," *The Pacific Historical Review,* II (March, 1933), 34–51.

George W. Pierson, "The Frontier and Frontiersman of Turner's Essays: A Scrutiny of the Foundations of the Middle Western Tradition," *The Pennsylvania Magazine of History and Biography,* LXIV (October, 1940), 449–478.

Robert E. Riegel, *America Moves West* (New York, 1947), ch. 40.

———, "Current Ideas of the Significance of the United States Frontier," *Revista de Historia de America,*" XXXIII (June, 1952), 25–43.

THE SIGNIFICANCE
OF THE FRONTIER
IN AMERICAN HISTORY

The Significance of the Frontier in American History

IN A RECENT bulletin of the Superintendent of the Census for 1890 appear these significant words: "Up to and including 1880 the country had a frontier of settlement, but at present the unsettled area has been so broken into by isolated bodies of settlement that there can hardly be said to be a frontier line. In the discussion of its extent, its westward movement, etc., it can not therefore, any longer have a place in the census reports." This brief official statement marks the closing of a great historic movement. Up to our own day American history has been in a large degree the history of the colonization of the Great West. The existence of an area of free land, its continuous recession, and the advance of American settlement westward, explain American development.

Behind institutions, behind constitutional forms and modifications, lie the vital forces that call these organs into life and shape them to meet changing conditions. The peculiarity of American institutions is, the fact that they have been compelled to adapt themselves to the changes of an expanding people—to the changes involved in crossing a continent, in winning a wilderness, and in developing at each area of this progress out of the primitive economic and political conditions of the frontier into the complexity of city life. Said Calhoun in 1817, "We are great, and rapidly— I was about to say fearfully—growing!" So saying, he touched the distinguishing feature of American life. All peoples show development; the germ theory of politics has been sufficiently emphasized. In the case of most nations, however,

Note: The text of Turner's essay is reprinted from *Annual Report for 1893*, American Historical Association, pp. 199–227. Turner's own punctuation and capitalization, except in a few instances, have been retained. The subheadings are those of the original essay.

the development has occurred in a limited area; and if the nation has expanded, it has met other growing peoples whom it has conquered. But in the case of the United States we have a different phenomenon. Limiting our attention to the Atlantic coast, we have the familiar phenomenon of the evolution of institutions in a limited area, such as the rise of representative government; the differentiation of simple colonial governments into complex organs; the progress from primitive industrial society, without division of labor, up to manufacturing civilization. But we have in addition to this a recurrence of the process of evolution in each western area reached in the process of expansion. Thus American development has exhibited not merely advance along a single line, but a return to primitive conditions on a continually advancing frontier line, and a new development for that area. American social development has been continually beginning over again on the frontier. This perennial rebirth, this fluidity of American life, this expansion westward with its new opportunities, its continuous touch with the simplicity of primitive society, furnish the forces dominating American character. The true point of view in the history of this nation is not the Atlantic coast, it is the great West. Even the slavery struggle, which is made so exclusive an object of attention by writers like Prof. von Holst, occupies its important place in American history because of its relation to westward expansion.

In this advance, the frontier is the outer edge of the wave—the meeting point between savagery and civilization. Much has been written about the frontier from the point of view of border warfare and the chase, but as a field for the serious study of the economist and the historian it has been neglected.

The American frontier is sharply distinguished from the European frontier—a fortified boundary line running through dense populations. The most significant thing about the American frontier is, that it lies at the hither edge of free land. In the census reports it is treated as the margin of that settlement which has a density of two or more to the square mile. The term is an elastic one, and for our purposes does not need sharp definition. We shall consider the whole frontier belt, including the Indian country and the outer margin of the "settled area" of the census reports. This paper will make no attempt to treat the subject exhaustively; its aim is simply to call attention to the frontier as a fertile field for investigation, and to suggest some of the problems which arise in connection with it.

In the settlement of America we have to observe how European life entered the continent, and how America modified and developed that life and reacted on Europe. Our early history is the study of European germs developing in an American environment. Too exclusive attention has been paid by institutional students to the Germanic origins, too little to the American factors. The frontier is the line of most rapid and effective Americanization. The wilderness masters the colonist. It finds him a European in dress, industries, tools, modes of travel, and thought. It takes him from the railroad car and puts him in the birch canoe. It strips off the garments of civilization and arrays him in the hunting shirt and the moccasin. It puts him in the log cabin of the Cherokee and Iroquois and runs an Indian palisade around him. Before long he has gone to planting Indian corn and plowing with a sharp stick; he shouts the war cry and takes the scalp in orthodox Indian fashion. In short, at the frontier the environment is at first too strong for the man. He must accept the conditions which it furnishes, or perish, and so he fits himself into the Indian clearings and follows the Indian trails. Little by little he transforms the wilderness, but the outcome is not the old Europe, not simply the development of Germanic germs, any more than the first phenomenon was a case of reversion to the Germanic mark. The fact is, that here is a new product that is American. At first, the frontier was the Atlantic coast. It was the frontier of Europe in a very real sense. Moving westward, the frontier became more and more American.

As successive terminal moraines result from successive glaciations, so each frontier leaves its traces behind it, and when it becomes a settled area the region still partakes of the frontier characteristics. Thus the advance of the frontier has meant a steady movement away from the influence of Europe, a steady growth of independence on American lines. And to study this advance, the men who grew up under these conditions, and the political, economic, and social results of it, is to study the really American part of our history.

Stages of frontier advance

In the course of the seventeenth century the frontier was advanced up the Atlantic river courses, just beyond the "fall line," and the tidewater region became the settled area. In the first half of the eighteenth century another advance occurred. Traders followed the Delaware and Shawnese Indians to the Ohio as early as the end of the first quarter of the century. Governor Spotswood of Virginia made an expedition in 1714 across the Blue Ridge. The end of the first quarter of the century saw the advance of the Scotch-Irish and the Palatine Germans up the Shenandoah Valley into the western part of Virginia, and along the Piedmont region of the Carolinas. The Germans in New York pushed the frontier of settlement up the Mohawk to German Flats. In Pennsylvania the town of Bedford indicates the line of settlement. Settlements had begun on New River, a branch of the Kanawha, and on the sources of the Yadkin and French Broad. The King attempted to arrest the advance by his proclamation of 1763, forbidding settlements beyond the sources of the rivers flowing into the Atlantic; but in vain. In the period of the Revolution the frontier crossed the Alleghanies into Kentucky and Tennessee, and the upper waters of the Ohio were settled. When the first census was taken in 1790, the continuous settled area was bounded by a line which ran near the coast of Maine, and

included New England except a portion of Vermont and
New Hampshire, New York along the Hudson and up the
Mohawk about Schenectady, eastern and southern Pennsylvania, Virginia well across the Shenandoah Valley, and the
Carolinas and eastern Georgia. Beyond this region of continuous settlement were the small settled areas of Kentucky
and Tennessee, and the Ohio, with the mountains interven-
ing between them and the Atlantic area, thus giving a new
and important character to the frontier. The isolation of the
region increased its peculiarly American tendencies, and the
need of transportation facilities to connect it with the East
called out important schemes of internal improvement,
which will be noted farther on. The "West," as a self-conscious section, began to evolve.

From decade to decade distinct advances of the frontier occurred. By the census of 1820 the settled area included
Ohio, southern Indiana and Illinois, southeastern Missouri,
and about one-half of Louisiana. This settled area had sur-
rounded Indian areas, and the management of these tribes
became an object of political concern. The frontier region
of the time lay along the Great Lakes, where Astor's American Fur Company operated in the Indian trade, and beyond
the Mississippi, where Indian traders extended their activity even to the Rocky Mountains; Florida also furnished
frontier conditions. The Mississippi River region was the
scene of typical frontier settlements.

The rising steam navigation on western waters, the
opening of the Erie Canal, and the westward extension of
cotton culture added five frontier states to the Union in this
period. Grund, writing in 1836, declares: "It appears then
that the universal disposition of Americans to emigrate to
the western wilderness, in order to enlarge their dominion
over inanimate nature, is the actual result of an expansive
power which is inherent in them, and which by continually
agitating all classes of society is constantly throwing a
large portion of the whole population on the extreme con-
fines of the State, in order to gain space for its develop-

ment. Hardly is a new State or Territory formed before the same principle manifests itself again and gives rise to a further emigration; and so is it destined to go on until a physical barrier must finally obstruct its progress."

In the middle of this century the line indicated by the present eastern boundary of Indian Territory, Nebraska, and Kansas marked the frontier of the Indian country. Minnesota and Wisconsin still exhibited frontier conditions, but the distinctive frontier of the period is found in California, where the gold discoveries had sent a sudden tide of adventurous miners, and in Oregon, and the settlements in Utah. As the frontier has leaped over the Alleghanies, so now it skipped the Great Plains and the Rocky Mountains; and in the same way that the advance of the frontiersmen beyond the Alleghanies had caused the rise of important questions of transportation and internal improvement, so now the settlers beyond the Rocky Mountains needed means of communication with the East, and in the furnishing of these arose the settlement of the Great Plains and the development of still another kind of frontier life. Railroads, fostered by land grants, sent an increasing tide of immigrants into the far West. The United States Army fought a series of Indian wars in Minnesota, Dakota, and the Indian Territory.

By 1880 the settled area had been pushed into northern Michigan, Wisconsin, and Minnesota, along Dakota rivers, and in the Black Hills region, and was ascending the rivers of Kansas and Nebraska. The development of mines in Colorado had drawn isolated frontier settlements into that region, and Montana and Idaho were receiving settlers. The frontier was found in these mining camps and the ranches of the Great Plains. The superintendent of the census for 1890 reports, as previously stated, that the settlements of the West lie so scattered over the region that there can no longer be said to be a frontier line.

In these successive frontiers we find natural boundary lines which have served to mark and to affect the characteristics of the frontiers, namely: The "fall line"; the Alleghany

Mountains; the Mississippi; the Missouri, where its direction approximates north and south; the line of the arid lands, approximately the ninety-ninth meridian; and the Rocky Mountains. The fall line marked the frontier of the seventeenth century; the Alleghanies that of the eighteenth; the Mississippi that of the first quarter of the nineteenth; the Missouri that of the middle of this century (omitting the California movement); and the belt of the Rocky Mountains and the arid tract, the present frontier. Each was won by a series of Indian wars.

The frontier furnishes a field for comparative study of social development

At the Atlantic frontier one can study the germs of processes repeated at each successive frontier. We have the complex European life sharply precipitated by the wilderness into the simplicity of primitive conditions. The first frontier had to meet its Indian question, its question of the disposition of the public domain, of the means of intercourse with older settlements, of the extension of political organization, of religious and educational activity. And the settlement of these and similar questions for one frontier served as a guide for the next. The American student needs not to go to the "prim little townships of Sleswick" for illustrations of the law of continuity and development. For example, he may study the origin of our land policies in the colonial land policy; he may see how the system grew by adapting the statutes to the customs of the successive frontiers. He may see how the mining experience in the lead regions of Wisconsin, Illinois, and Iowa was applied to the mining laws of the Rockies, and how our Indian policy has been a series of experimentations on successive frontiers. Each tier of new States has found in the older ones material for its constitutions. Each frontier has made similar contributions to American character, as will be discussed farther on.

But with all these similarities there are essential differences, due to the place element and the time element. It is evident that the farming frontier of the Mississippi Valley presents different conditions from the mining frontier of the Rocky Mountains. The frontier reached by the Pacific Railroad, surveyed into rectangles, guarded by the United States Army, and recruited by the daily immigrant ship, moves forward at a swifter pace and in a different way than the frontier reached by the birch canoe or the pack horse. The geologist traces patiently the shores of ancient seas, maps their areas, and compares the older and the newer. It would be a work worth the historian's labors to mark these various frontiers and in detail compare one with another. Not only would there result a more adequate conception of American development and characteristics, but invaluable additions would be made to the history of society.

Loria, the Italian economist, has urged the study of colonial life as an aid in understanding the stages of European development, affirming that colonial settlement is for economic science what the mountain is for geology, bringing to light primitive stratifications. "America," he says, "has the key to the historical enigma which Europe has sought for centuries in vain, and the land which has no history reveals luminously the course of universal history." There is much truth in this. The United States lies like a huge page in the history of society. Line by line as we read this continental page from west to east we find the record of social evolution. It begins with the Indian and the hunter; it goes on to tell of the disintegration of savagery by the entrance of the trader, the pathfinder of civilization; we read the annals of the pastoral stage in ranch life; the exploitation of the soil by the raising of unrotated crops of corn and wheat in sparsely settled farming communities; the intensive culture of the denser farm settlement; and finally the manufacturing organization with city and factory system. This page is familiar to the student of census statistics, but how little of it has been used by our historians. Particularly in eastern

States this page is a palimpsest. What is now a manufacturing State was in an earlier decade an area of intensive farming. Earlier yet it had been a wheat area, and still earlier the "range" had attracted the cattle herder. Thus Wisconsin, now developing manufacture, is a State with varied agricultural interests. But earlier it was given over to almost exclusive grain-raising, like North Dakota at the present time.

Each of these areas has had an influence in our economic and political history; the evolution of each into a higher stage has worked political transformations. But what constitutional historian has made any adequate attempt to interpret political facts by the light of these social areas and changes?

The Atlantic frontier was compounded of fisherman, fur-trader, miner, cattle-raiser, and farmer. Excepting the fisherman, each type of industry was on the march toward the West, impelled by an irresistible attraction. Each passed in successive waves across the continent. Stand at Cumberland Gap and watch the procession of civilization, marching single file—the buffalo following the trail to the salt springs, the Indian, the fur-trader and hunter, the cattle-raiser, the pioneer farmer—and the frontier has passed by. Stand at South Pass in the Rockies a century later and see the same procession with wider intervals between. The unequal rate of advance compels us to distinguish the frontier into the trader's frontier, the rancher's frontier, or the miner's frontier, and the farmer's frontier. When the mines and the cow pens were still near the fall line the traders' pack trains were tinkling across the Alleghanies, and the French on the Great Lakes were fortifying their posts, alarmed by the British trader's birch canoe. When the trappers scaled the Rockies, the farmer was still near the mouth of the Missouri.

The Indian trader's frontier

Why was it that the Indian trader passed so rapidly across the continent? What effects followed from the trader's frontier? The trade was coeval with American discovery. The Norsemen, Vespuccius, Verrazani, Hudson, John Smith, all trafficked for furs. The Plymouth pilgrims settled in Indian cornfields, and their first return cargo was of beaver and lumber. The records of the various New England colonies show how steadily exploration was carried into the wilderness by this trade. What is true for New England is, as would be expected, even plainer for the rest of the colonies. All along the coast from Maine to Georgia the Indian trade opened up the river courses. Steadily the trader passed westward, utilizing the older lines of French trade. The Ohio, the Great Lakes, the Mississippi, the Missouri, and the Platte, the lines of western advance, were ascended by traders. They found the passes in the Rocky Mountains and guided Lewis and Clark, Fremont, and Bidwell. The explanation of the rapidity of this advance is connected with the effects of the trader on the Indian. The trading post left the unarmed tribes at the mercy of those that had purchased fire-arms—a truth which the Iroquois Indians wrote in blood, and so the remote and unvisited tribes gave eager welcome to the trader. "The savages," wrote La Salle, "take better care of us French than of their own children; from us only can they get guns and goods." This accounts for the trader's power and the rapidity of his advance. Thus the disintegrating forces of civilization entered the wilderness. Every river valley and Indian trail became a fissure in Indian society, and so that society became honeycombed. Long before the pioneer farmer appeared on the scene, primitive Indian life had passed away. The farmers met Indians armed with guns. The trading frontier, while steadily undermining Indian power by making the tribes ultimately dependent on the whites, yet, through its sale of guns, gave to the Indians increased power of resistance to the farming frontier. French colonization was dominated by its trading frontier; English colonization by its farming frontier. There was an antagonism between the two frontiers as between the two nations. Said Duquesne to the Iroquois, "Are you ignorant of the difference between the king of England and the king of France? Go see the forts that our king has established and you will see that you can still hunt under their very walls. They have been placed for your advantage in places which you frequent. The English, on the contrary, are no sooner in possession of a place than the game is driven away. The forest falls before them as they advance, and the soil is laid bare so that you can scarce find the wherewithal to erect a shelter for the night."

And yet, in spite of this opposition of the interests of the trader and the farmer, the Indian trade pioneered the way for civilization. The buffalo trail became the Indian trail, and this became the trader's "trace"; the trails widened into roads, and the roads into turnpikes, and these in turn were transformed into railroads. The same origin can be shown for the railroads of the South, the far West, and the Dominion of Canada. The trading posts reached by these trails were on the sites of Indian villages which had been placed in positions suggested by nature; and these trading posts, situated so as to command the water systems of the country, have grown into such cities as Albany, Pittsburgh, Detroit, Chicago, St. Louis, Council Bluffs, and Kansas City. Thus civilization in America has followed the arteries made by geology, pouring an ever richer tide through them, until at last the slender paths of aboriginal intercourse have been broadened and interwoven into the complex mazes of modern commercial lines; the wilderness has been interpenetrated by lines of civilization growing ever more numerous. It is like the steady growth of a complex nervous system for the originally simple, inert continent. If one would understand why we are to-day one nation, rather than a collection of isolated states, he must study this economic and social consolidation of the country. In this progress from savage conditions lie topics for the evolutionist.

The effect of the Indian frontier as a consolidating agent in our history is important. From the close of the seventeenth century various intercolonial congresses have been called to treat with Indians and establish common measures of defense. Particularism was strongest in colonies with no Indian frontier. This frontier stretched along the western border like a cord of union. The Indian was a common danger, demanding united action. Most celebrated of these conferences was the Albany congress of 1754, called to treat with the Six Nations, and to consider plans of union. Even a cursory reading of the plan proposed by the congress reveals the importance of the frontier. The powers of the general council and the officers were, chiefly, the determination of peace and war with the Indians, the regulation of Indian trade, the purchase of Indian lands, and the creation and government of new settlements as a security against the Indians. It is evident that the unifying tendencies of the Revolutionary period were facilitated by the previous co-operation in the regulation of the frontier. In this connection may be mentioned the importance of the frontier, from that day to this, as a military training school, keeping alive the power of resistance to aggression, and developing the stalwart and rugged qualities of the frontiersman.

The rancher's frontier

It would not be possible in the limits of this paper to trace the other frontiers across the continent. Travelers of the eighteenth century found the "cowpens" among the canebrakes and peavine pastures of the South, and the "cow drivers" took their droves to Charleston, Philadelphia, and New York. Travelers at the close of the War of 1812 met droves of more than a thousand cattle and swine from the interior of Ohio going to Pennsylvania to fatten for the Philadelphia market. The ranges of the Great Plains, with ranch and cowboy and nomadic life, are things of yesterday and of to-day. The experience of the Carolina cowpens guided the ranchers of Texas. One element favoring the rapid extension of the rancher's frontier is the fact that in a remote country lacking transportation facilities the product must be in small bulk, or must be able to transport itself, and the cattle raiser could easily drive his product to market. The effect of these great ranches on the subsequent agrarian history of the localities in which they existed should be studied.

The farmer's frontier

The maps of the census reports show an uneven advance of the farmer's frontier, with tongues of settlement pushed forward and with indentations of wilderness. In part this is due to Indian resistance, in part to the location of river valleys and passes, in part to the unequal force of the centers of frontier attraction. Among the important centers of attraction may be mentioned the following: fertile and favorably situated soils, salt springs, mines, and army posts.

Army posts

The frontier army post, serving to protect the settlers from the Indians, has also acted as a wedge to open the Indian country, and has been a nucleus for settlement. In this connection mention should also be made of the Government military and exploring expeditions in determining the lines of settlement. But all the more important expeditions were greatly indebted to the earliest pathmakers, the Indian guides, the traders and trappers, and the French voyageurs, who were inevitable parts of governmental expeditions from the days of Lewis and Clark. Each expedition was an epitome of the previous factors in western advance.

Salt springs

In an interesting monograph, Victor Hehn has traced the effect of salt upon early European development, and has pointed out how it affected the lines of settlement and the form of administration. A similar study might be made for the salt springs of the United States. The early settlers were tied to the coast by the need of salt, without which they could not preserve their meats or live in comfort. Writing in 1752, Bishop Spangenburg says of a colony for which he was seeking lands in North Carolina, "They will require salt & other necessaries which they can neither manufacture nor raise. Either they must go to Charleston, which is 300 miles distant . . . Or else they must go to Boling's Point in Vᵃ on a branch of the James & is also 300 miles from here . . . Or else they must go down the Roanoke—I know not how many miles—where salt is brought up from the Cape Fear." This may serve as a typical illustration. An annual pilgrimage to the coast for salt thus became essential. Taking flocks or furs and ginseng root, the early settlers sent their pack trains after seeding time each year to the coast. This proved to be an important educational influence, since it was almost the only way in which the pioneer learned what was going on in the East. But when discovery was made of the salt springs of the Kanawha, and the Holston, and Kentucky, and central New York, the West began to be freed from dependence on the coast. It was in part the effect of finding these salt springs that enabled settlement to cross the mountains.

From the time the mountains rose between the pioneer and the seaboard, a new order of Americanism arose. The West and the East began to get out of touch of each other. The settlements from the sea to the mountains kept connection with the rear and had a certain solidarity. But the over-mountain men grew more and more independent. The East took a narrow view of American advance, and nearly lost these men. Kentucky and Tennessee history bears abundant witness to the truth of this statement. The East began to try to hedge and limit westward expansion. Though Webster could declare that there were no Alleghanies in his politics, yet in politics in general they were a very solid factor.

Land

The exploitation of the beasts took hunter and trader to the west, the exploitation of the grasses took the rancher west, and the exploitation of the virgin soil of the river valleys and prairies attracted the farmer. Good soils have been the most continuous attraction to the farmer's frontier. The land hunger of the Virginians drew them down the rivers into Carolina, in early colonial days; the search for soils took the Massachusetts men to Pennsylvania and to New York. As the eastern lands were taken up migration flowed across them to the west. Daniel Boone, the great backwoodsman, who combined the occupations of hunter, trader, cattle raiser, farmer, and surveyor—learning, probably from the traders, of the fertility of the lands on the upper Yadkin, where the traders were wont to rest as they took their way to the Indians, left his Pennsylvania home with his father, and passed down the Great Valley road to that stream. Learning from a trader whose posts were on the Red River in Kentucky of its game and rich pastures, he pioneered the way for the farmers to that region. Thence he passed to the frontier of Missouri, where his settlement was long a landmark on the frontier. Here again he helped to open the way for civilization, finding salt licks, and trails, and land. His son was among the earliest trappers in the passes of the Rocky Mountains, and his party are said to have been the first to camp on the present site of Denver. His grandson, Col. A. J. Boone, of Colorado, was a power among the Indians of the Rocky Mountains, and was appointed an agent by the Government. Kit Carson's mother was a Boone. Thus this family epitomizes the backwoodsman's advance across the continent.

The farmer's advance came in a distinct series of waves. In Peck's New Guide to the West, published in Boston in 1837, occurs this suggestive passage:

> Generally, in all the western settlements, three classes, like the waves of the ocean, have rolled one after the other. First

comes the pioneer, who depends for the subsistence of his family chiefly upon the natural growth of vegetation, called the "range," and the proceeds of hunting. His implements of agriculture are rude, chiefly of his own make, and his efforts directed mainly to a crop of corn and a "truck patch." The last is a rude garden for growing cabbage, beans, corn for roasting ears, cucumbers, and potatoes. A log cabin and, occasionally, a stable and corn-crib, and a field of a dozen acres, the timber girdled or "deadened," and fenced, are enough for his occupancy. It is quite immaterial whether he ever becomes the owner of the soil. He is the occupant for the time being, pays no rent, and feels as independent as the "lord of the manor." With a horse, cow, and one or two breeders of swine, he strikes into the woods with his family, and becomes the founder of a new county, or perhaps state. He builds his cabin, gathers around him a few other families of similar tastes and habits, and occupies till the range is somewhat subdued, and hunting a little precarious, or, which is more frequently the case, till the neighbors crowd around, roads, bridges, and fields annoy him, and he lacks elbow room. The preemption law enables him to dispose of his cabin and cornfield to the next class of emigrants; and, to employ his own figures, he "breaks for the high timber," "clears out for the New Purchase," or migrates to Arkansas or Texas, to work the same process over.

The next class of emigrants purchase the lands, add field to field, clear out the roads, throw rough bridges over the streams, put up hewn log houses with glass windows and brick or stone chimneys, occasionally plant orchards, build mills, schoolhouses, court-houses, etc., and exhibit the picture and forms of plain frugal, civilized life.

Another wave rolls on. The men of capital and enterprise come. The settler is ready to sell out and take the advantage of the rise in property, push farther into the interior and become, himself, a man of capital and enterprise in turn. The small village rises to a spacious town or city; substantial edifices of brick, extensive fields, orchards, gardens, colleges, and churches are seen. Broadcloths, silks, leghorns, crapes, and all the refinements, luxuries, elegancies, frivolities, and fashions are in vogue. Thus wave after wave is rolling westward; the real Eldorado is still farther on.

A portion of the two first classes remain stationary amidst the general movement, improve their habits and condition, and rise in the scale of society.

The writer has traveled much amongst the first class, the real pioneers. He has lived many years in connection with the second grade; and now the third wave is sweeping over large districts of Indiana, Illinois, and Missouri. Migration has become almost a habit in the West. Hundreds of men can be found, not over 50 years of age, who have settled for the fourth, fifth, or sixth time on a new spot. To sell out and remove only a few hundred miles makes up a portion of the variety of backwoods life and manners.

Omitting those of the pioneer farmers who move from the love of adventure, the advance of the more steady farmer is easy to understand. Obviously the immigrant was attracted by the cheap lands of the frontier, and even the native farmer felt their influence strongly. Year by year the farmers who lived on soil whose returns were diminished by unrotated crops were offered the virgin soil of the frontier at nominal prices. Their growing families demanded more lands, and these were dear. The competition of the unexhausted, cheap, and easily tilled prairie lands compelled the farmer either to go west and continue the exhaustion of the soil on a new frontier, or to adopt intensive culture. Thus the census of 1890 shows, in the Northwest, many counties in which there is an absolute or a relative decrease of population. These States have been sending farmers to advance the frontier on the plains, and have themselves begun to turn to intensive farming and to manufacture. A decade before this, Ohio had shown the same transition stage. Thus the demand for land and the love of wilderness freedom drew the frontier ever onward.

Having now roughly outlined the various kinds of frontiers, and their modes of advance, chiefly from the point of view of the frontier itself, we may next inquire what were the influences on the East and on the Old World. A rapid enumeration of some of the more noteworthy effects is all that I have time for.

Composite nationality

First, we note that the frontier promoted the formation of a composite nationality for the American people. The coast was preponderantly English, but the later tides of continental immigration flowed across to the free lands. This was the case from the early colonial days. The Scotch-Irish and the Palatine Germans, or "Pennsylvania Dutch," furnished the dominant element in the stock of the colonial frontier. With these peoples were also the freed indented servants, or redemptioners, who at the expiration of their time of service passed to the frontier. Governor Spottswood of Virginia writes in 1717, "The inhabitants of our frontiers are composed generally of such as have been transported hither as servants, and, being out of their time, settle themselves where land is to be taken up and that will produce the necessarys of life with little labour." Very generally these redemptioners were of non-English stock. In the crucible of the frontier the immigrants were Americanized, liberated, and fused into a mixed race, English in neither nationality nor characteristics. The process has gone on from the early days to our own. Burke and other writers in the middle of the eighteenth century believed that Pennsylvania was "threatened with the danger of being wholly foreign in language, manners, and perhaps even inclinations." The German and Scotch-Irish elements in the frontier of the South were only less great. In the middle of the present century the German element in Wisconsin was already so considerable that leading publicists looked to the creation of a German state out of the commonwealth by concentrating their colonization. Such examples teach us to beware

THE SIGNIFICANCE OF THE FRONTIER 45

of misinterpreting the fact that there is a common English speech in America into a belief that the stock is also English.

Industrial independence

In another way the advance of the frontier decreased our dependence on England. The coast, particularly of the South, lacked diversified industries, and was dependent on England for the bulk of its supplies. In the South there was even a dependence on the Northern colonies for articles of food. Governor Glenn, of South Carolina, writes in the middle of the eighteenth century: "Our trade with New York and Philadelphia was of this sort, draining us of all the little money and bills we could gather from other places for their bread, flour, beer, hams, bacon, and other things of their produce, all which, except beer, our new townships begin to supply us with, which are settled with very industrious and thriving Germans. This no doubt diminishes the number of shipping and the appearance of our trade, but it is far from being a detriment to us." Before long the frontier created a demand for merchants. As it retreated from the coast it became less and less possible for England to bring her supplies directly to the consumer's wharfs, and carry away staple crops, and staple crops began to give way to diversified agriculture for a time. The effect of this phase of the frontier action upon the northern section is perceived when we realize how the advance of the frontier aroused seaboard cities like Boston, New York, and Baltimore, to engage in rivalry for what Washington called "the extensive and valuable trade of a rising empire."

Effects on national legislation

The legislation which most developed the powers of the National Government, and played the largest part in its activity, was conditioned on the frontier. Writers have discussed the subjects of tariff, land, and internal improvement, as subsidiary to the slavery question. But when American history comes to be rightly viewed it will be seen that the slavery question is an incident. In the period from the end of the first half of the present century to the close of the civil war slavery rose to primary, but far from exclusive, importance. But this does not justify Dr. von Holst (to take an example) in treating our constitutional history in its formative period down to 1828 in a single volume, giving six volumes chiefly to the history of slavery from 1828 to 1861, under the title "Constitutional History of the United States." The growth of nationalism and the evolution of American political institutions were dependent on the advance of the frontier. Even so recent a writer as Rhodes, in his "History of the United States since the Compromise of 1850," has treated the legislation called out by the western advance as incidental to the slavery struggle.

This is a wrong perspective. The pioneer needed the goods of the coast, and so the grand series of internal improvement and railroad legislation began, with potent nationalizing effects. Over internal improvements occurred great debates, in which grave constitutional questions were discussed. Sectional groupings appear in the votes, profoundly significant for the historian. Loose construction increased as the nation marched westward. But the West was not content with bringing the farm to the factory. Under the lead of Clay—"Harry of the West"—protective tariffs were passed, with the cry of bringing the factory to the farm. The disposition of the public lands was a third important subject of national legislation influenced by the frontier.

The public domain

The public domain has been a force of profound importance in the nationalization and development of the Government. The effects of the struggle of the landed and the landless States, and of the ordinance of 1787, need no discussion. Administratively the frontier called out some of the highest and most vitalizing activities of the General Government. The purchase of Louisiana was perhaps the constitutional turning point in the history of the Republic, inasmuch as it afforded both a new area for national legislation and the occasion of the downfall of the policy of strict construction. But the purchase of Louisiana was called out by frontier needs and demands. As frontier States accrued to the Union the national power grew. In a speech on the dedication of the Calhoun monument Mr. Lamar explained: "In 1789 the States were the creators of the Federal Government; in 1861 the Federal Government was the creator of a large majority of the States."

When we consider the public domain from the point of view of the sale and disposal of the public lands we are again brought face to face with the frontier. The policy of the United States in dealing with its lands is in sharp contrast with the European system of scientific administration. Efforts to make this domain a source of revenue, and to withhold it from emigrants in order that settlement might be compact, were in vain. The jealousy and the fears of the East were powerless in the face of the demands of the frontiersmen. John Quincy Adams was obliged to confess: "My own system of administration, which was to make the national domain the inexhaustible fund for progressive and unceasing internal improvement, has failed." The reason is obvious; a system of administration was not what the West demanded; it wanted land. Adams states the situation as follows: "The slaveholders of the South have bought the cooperation of the western country by the bribe of the western lands, abandoning to the new Western States their own proportion of the public property and aiding them in the design of grasping all the lands into their own hands. Thomas H. Benton was the author of this system, which he brought forward as a substitute for the American system of Mr. Clay, and to supplant him as the leading statesman of the West. Mr. Clay, by his tariff compromise with Mr. Calhoun, abandoned his own American system. At the same time he brought forward a plan for distributing among all the States of the Union the proceeds of the sales of the public lands. His bill for that purpose passed both Houses of Congress, but was vetoed by President Jackson, who, in his annual message of December, 1832, formally recommended that all public lands should be gratuitously given away to individual adventurers and to the States in which the lands are situated.

"No subject," said Henry Clay, "which has presented itself to the present, or perhaps any preceding, Congress, is of greater magnitude than that of the public lands." When we consider the far-reaching effects of the Government's land policy upon political, economic, and social aspects of American life, we are disposed to agree with him. But this legislation was framed under frontier influences, and under the lead of Western statesmen like Benton and Jackson. Said Senator Scott of Indiana in 1841: "I consider the pre-emption law merely declaratory of the custom or common law of the settlers."

National tendencies of the frontier

It is safe to say that the legislation with regard to land, tariff, and internal improvements—the American system of the nationalizing Whig party—was conditioned on frontier ideas and needs. But it was not merely in legislative action that the frontier worked against the sectionalism of the coast. The economic and social characteristics of the frontier worked against sectionalism. The men of the frontier had closer resemblances to the Middle region than to either of the other sections. Pennsylvania had been the seed-plot of frontier emigration, and, although she passed on her settlers along the Great Valley into the west of Virginia and the Carolinas, yet the industrial society of these Southern frontiersmen was always more like that of the Middle region

than like that of the tide-water portion of the South, which
later came to spread its industrial type throughout the
South.

The Middle region, entered by New York harbor, was
an open door to all Europe. The tide-water part of the
South represented typical Englishmen, modified by a warm
climate and servile labor, and living in baronial fashion on
great plantations; New England stood for a special English
movement—Puritanism. The Middle region was less English
than the other sections. It had a wide mixture of nationali-
ties, a varied society, the mixed town and county system of
local government, a varied economic life, many religious
sects. In short, it was a region mediating between New
England and the South, and the East and the West. It
represented that composite nationality which the contem-
porary United States exhibits, that juxtaposition of non-
English groups, occupying a valley or a little settlement,
and presenting reflections of the map of Europe in their
variety. It was typical of the modern United States. It was
least sectional, not only because it lay between North and
South, but also because with no barriers to shut out its
frontiers from its settled region, and with a system of con-
necting waterways, the Middle region mediated between
East and West as well as between North and South. Thus
it became the typically American region. Even the New
Englander, who was shut out from the frontier by the Middle region, tarrying in New York or Pennsylvania on his
westward march, lost the acuteness of his sectionalism on
the way.

The spread of cotton culture into the interior of the
South finally broke down the contrast between the "tide-
water" region and the rest of the State, and based Southern
interests on slavery. Before this process revealed its results
the western portion of the South, which was akin to Pennsylvania in stock, society, and industry, showed tendencies
to fall away from the faith of the fathers into internal improvement legislation and nationalism. In the Virginia con-

vention of 1829–30, called to revise the constitution, Mr. Leigh, of Chesterfield, one of the tide-water counties, declared:

> One of the main causes of discontent which led to this convention, that which had the strongest influence in overcoming our veneration for the work of our fathers, which taught us to contemn the sentiments of Henry and Mason and Pendleton, which weaned us from our reverence for the constituted authorities of the State, was an overweening passion for internal improvement. I say this with perfect knowledge, for it has been avowed to me by gentlemen from the West over and over again. And let me tell the gentleman from Albemarle (Mr. Gordon) that it has been another principal object of those who set this ball of revolution in motion, to overturn the doctrine of State rights, of which Virginia has been the very pillar, and to remove the barrier she has interposed to the interference of the Federal Government in that same work of internal improvement, by so reorganizing the legislature that Virginia, too, may be hitched to the Federal car.

It was this nationalizing tendency of the West that transformed the democracy of Jefferson into the national republicanism of Monroe and the democracy of Andrew Jackson. The West of the War of 1812, the West of Clay, and Benton, and Harrison, and Andrew Jackson, shut off by the Middle States and the mountains from the coast sections, had a solidarity of its own with national tendencies. On the tide of the Father of Waters, North and South met and mingled into a nation. Interstate migration went steadily on—a process of cross-fertilization of ideas and institutions. The fierce struggle of the sections over slavery on the western frontier does not diminish the truth of this statement; it proves the truth of it. Slavery was a sectional trait that would not down, but in the West it could not remain sectional. It was the greatest of frontiersmen who declared: "I believe this Government can not endure permanently half slave and half free. It will become all of one thing or all of the other." Nothing works for nationalism like intercourse within the nation. Mobility of population is death to localism, and the western frontier worked irresistibly in unsettling population. The effects reached back from the frontier and affected profoundly the Atlantic coast and even the Old World.

Growth of democracy

But the most important effect of the frontier has been in the promotion of democracy here and in Europe. As has been indicated, the frontier is productive of individualism. Complex society is precipitated by the wilderness into a kind of primitive organization based on the family. The tendency is anti-social. It produces antipathy to control, and particularly to any direct control. The tax gatherer is viewed as a representative of oppression. Professor Osgood, in an able article, has pointed out that the frontier conditions prevalent in the colonies are important factors in the explanation of the American Revolution, where individual liberty was sometimes confused with absence of all effective government. The same conditions aid in explaining the difficulty of instituting a strong government in the period of the confederacy. The frontier individualism has from the beginning promoted democracy.

The frontier States that came into the Union in the first quarter of a century of its existence came in with democratic suffrage provisions, and had reactive effects of the highest importance upon the older States whose peoples were being attracted there. An extension of the franchise became essential. It was *western* New York that forced an extension of suffrage in the constitutional convention of that State in 1821; and it was *western* Virginia that compelled the tide-water region to put a more liberal suffrage provision in the constitution framed in 1830, and to give to the frontier region a more nearly proportionate representation with the tide-water aristocracy. The rise of democracy as an effective force in the nation came in with western preponderance under Jackson and William Henry Harrison, and it meant the triumph of the frontier—with all of its good and with all of its evil elements. An interesting illustration of the tone of frontier democracy in 1830 comes from the same debates in the Virginia convention already referred to. A representative from western Virginia declared:

> But, sir, it is not the increase of population in the West which this gentleman ought to fear. It is the energy which the mountain breeze and western habits impart to those emigrants. They are regenerated, politically I mean, sir. They soon become *working politicians;* and the difference, sir, between a *talking* and a *working* politician is immense. The Old Dominion has long been celebrated for producing great orators; the ablest metaphysicians in policy; men that can split hairs in all abstruse questions of political economy. But at home, or when they return from Congress, they have negroes to fan them asleep. But a Pennsylvania, a New York, an Ohio, or a western Virginia statesman, though far inferior in logic, metaphysics, and rhetoric to an old Virginia statesman, has this advantage, that when he returns home he takes off his coat and takes hold of the plow. This gives him bone and muscle, sir, and preserves his republican principles pure and uncontaminated.

So long as free land exists, the opportunity for a competency exists, and economic power secures political power. But the democracy born of free land, strong in selfishness and individualism, intolerant of administrative experience and education, and pressing individual liberty beyond its proper bounds, has its dangers as well as its benefits. Individualism in America has allowed a laxity in regard to governmental affairs which has rendered possible the spoils system and all the manifest evils that follow from the lack of a highly developed civic spirit. In this connection may be noted also the influence of frontier conditions in permitting lax business honor, inflated paper currency and wild-cat banking. The colonial and revolutionary frontier was the region whence emanated many of the worst forms of an evil currency. The West in the War of 1812 repeated the phenomenon on the frontier of that day, while the speculation and the wild-cat banking of the period of the crisis of 1837 occurred on the new frontier belt of the next tier of States. Thus each one of the periods of lax financial integrity coincides with periods when a new set of frontier communities had arisen, and coincides in area with these successive frontiers, for the most part. The recent Populist agitation is a case in point. Many a State that now declines any connection with the tenets of the Populists, itself adhered to such ideas in an earlier stage of the development of the State. A primitive society can hardly be expected to show the intelligent appreciation of the complexity of business interests in a developed society. The continual recurrence of these areas of paper-money agitation is another evidence that the frontier can be isolated and studied as a factor in American history of the highest importance.

Attempts to check and regulate the frontier

The East has always feared the result of an unregulated advance of the frontier, and has tried to check and guide it. The English authorities would have checked settlement at the headwaters of the Atlantic tributaries and allowed the "savages to enjoy their deserts in quiet lest the peltry trade should decrease." This called out Burke's splendid protest:

> If you stopped your grants, what would be the consequence? The people would occupy without grants. They have already so occupied in many places. You can not station garrisons in every part of these deserts. If you drive the people from one place, they will carry on their annual tillage and remove with their flocks and herds to another.

Many of the people in the back settlements are already little attached to particular situations. Already they have topped the Appalachian mountains. From thence they behold before them an immense plain, one vast, rich, level meadow; a square of five hundred miles. Over this they would wander without a possibility of restraint; they would change their manners with their habits of life; would soon forget a government by which they were disowned; would become hordes of English Tartars; and, pouring down upon your unfortified frontiers a fierce and irresistible cavalry, become masters of your governors and your counselors, your collectors and comptrollers, and of all the slaves that adhered to them. Such would, and in no long time must, be the effect of attempting to forbid as a crime and to suppress as an evil the command and blessing of Providence, "Increase and multiply." Such would be the happy result of an endeavor to keep as a lair of wild beasts that earth which God, by an express charter, has given to the children of men.

But the English Government was not alone in its desire to limit the advance of the frontier and guide its destinies. Tide-water Virginia and South Carolina gerrymandered those colonies to insure the dominance of the coast in their legislatures. Washington desired to settle a State at a time in the Northwest; Jefferson would reserve from settlement the territory of his Louisiana purchase north of the thirty-second parallel, in order to offer it to the Indians in exchange for their settlements east of the Mississippi. "When we shall be full on this side," he writes, "we may lay off a range of States on the western bank from the head to the mouth, and so range after range, advancing compactly as we multiply." Madison went so far as to argue to the French minister that the United States had no interest in seeing population extend itself on the right bank of the Mississippi, but should rather fear it. When the Oregon question was under debate, in 1824, Smyth, of Virginia, would draw an unchangeable line for the limits of the United States at the outer limit of two tiers of States beyond the Mississippi, complaining that the seaboard States were being drained of the flower of their population by the bringing of too much land into market. Even Thomas Benton, the man of widest views of the destiny of the West, at this stage of his career declared that along the ridge of the Rocky mountains "the western limits of the Republic should be drawn, and the statue of the fabled god Terminus should be raised upon its highest peak, never to be thrown down." But the attempts to limit the boundaries, to restrict land sales and settlement, and to deprive the West of its share of political power were all in vain. Steadily the frontier of settlement advanced and carried with it individualism, democracy, and nationalism, and powerfully affected the East and the Old World.

Missionary activity

The most effective efforts of the East to regulate the frontier came through its educational and religious activity, exerted by interstate migration and by organized societies. Speaking in 1835, Dr. Lyman Beecher declared: "It is equally plain that the religious and political destiny of our nation is to be decided in the West," and he pointed out that the population of the West "is assembled from all the States of the Union and from all the nations of Europe, and is rushing in like the waters of the flood, demanding for its moral preservation the immediate and universal action of those institutions which discipline the mind and arm the conscience and the heart. And so various are the opinions and habits, and so recent and imperfect is the acquaintance, and so sparse are the settlements of the West, that no homogeneous public sentiment can be formed to legislate immediately into being the requisite institutions. And yet they are all needed immediately in their utmost perfection and power. A nation is being 'born in a day.' . . . But what will become of the West if her prosperity rushes up to such a majesty of power, while those great institutions linger which are necessary to form the mind and the conscience and the heart of that vast world? It must not be permitted. . . . Let no man at the East quiet himself and dream of liberty, whatever may become of the West. . . . Her destiny is our destiny."

With the appeal to the conscience of New England, he adds appeals to her fears lest other religious sects anticipate her own. The New England preacher and school-teacher left their mark on the West. The dread of Western emancipation from New England's political and economic control was paralleled by her fears lest the West cut loose from her religion. Commenting in 1850 on reports that settlement was rapidly extending northward in Wisconsin, the editor of the Home Missionary writes: "We scarcely know whether to rejoice or mourn over this extension of our settlements. While we sympathize in whatever tends to increase the physical resources and prosperity of our country, we can not forget that with all these dispersions into remote and still remoter corners of the land the supply of the means of grace is becoming relatively less and less." Acting in accordance with such ideas, home missions were established and Western colleges were erected. As seaboard cities like Philadelphia, New York, and Baltimore strove for the mastery of Western trade, so the various denominations strove for the possession of the West. Thus an intellectual stream from New England sources fertilized the West. Other sections sent their missionaries; but the real struggle was between sects. The contest for power and the expansive tendency furnished to the various sects by the existence of a moving frontier must have had important results on the character of religious organization in the United States. The multiplication of rival churches in the little frontier towns had deep and lasting social effects. The religious aspects of the frontier make a chapter in our history which needs study.

Intellectual traits

From the conditions of frontier life came intellectual traits of profound importance. The works of travelers along each frontier from colonial days onward describe certain common traits, and these traits have, while softening down, still persisted as survivals in the place of their origin, even when a higher social organization succeeded. The result is that to the frontier the American intellect owes its striking characteristics. That coarseness and strength combined with acuteness and inquisitiveness; that practical, inventive turn of mind, quick to find expedients; that masterful grasp of material things, lacking in the artistic but powerful to effect great ends; that restless, nervous energy; that dominant individualism, working for good and for evil, and withal that buoyancy and exuberance which comes with freedom—these are traits of the frontier, or traits called out elsewhere because of the existence of the frontier. Since the days when the fleet of Columbus sailed into the waters of the New World, America has been another name for opportunity, and the people of the United States have taken their tone from the incessant expansion which has not only been open but has even been forced upon them. He would be a rash prophet who should assert that the expansive character of American life has now entirely ceased. Movement has been its dominant fact, and, unless this training has no effect upon a people, the American energy will continually demand a wider field for its exercise. But never again will such gifts of free land offer themselves. For a moment, at the frontier, the bonds of custom are broken and unrestraint is triumphant. There is not *tabula rasa*. The stubborn American environment is there with its imperious summons to accept its conditions; the inherited ways of doing things are also there; and yet, in spite of environment, and in spite of custom, each frontier did indeed furnish a new field of opportunity, a gate of escape from the bondage of the past;

and freshness, and confidence, and scorn of older society, impatience of its restraints and its ideas, and indifference to its lessons, have accompanied the frontier. What the Mediterranean Sea was to the Greeks, breaking the bond of custom, offering new experiences, calling out new institutions and activities, that, and more, the ever retreating frontier has been to the United States directly, and to the nations of Europe more remotely. And now, four centuries from the discovery of America, at the end of a hundred years of life under the Constitution, the frontier has gone, and with its going has closed the first period of American history.